BRIAN PAUL HINDLE

MEDIEVAL TOWN PLANS

SHIRE ARCHAEOLOGY

Cover photograph
Elm Hill, Norwich. This street was known as
Hundegate in medieval times.
(Photograph: Paul Hindle.)
British Library Cataloguing in Publication Data:
Hindle, Brian Paul.
Medieval town plans.
1. England. Towns, history.
I. Title.
942. 009732.
ISBN 0-7478-0065-0.

Published by
SHIRE PUBLICATIONS LTD
Cromwell House, Church Street, Princes Risborough,
Buckinghamshire HP17 9AJ, UK.

Series Editor: James Dyer.

ISBN 0 7478 0065 0.

First published 1990.

Printed in Great Britain by
C. I. Thomas & Sons (Haverfordwest) Ltd,
Press Buildings, Merlins Bridge, Haverfordwest, Dyfed SA61 1XF.

Contents

4

List of illustrations

Acknowledgements

I am extremely grateful to all the people who have allowed me to use illustrative material. In particular I must thank Dyfed Record Office, Lovell Johns Limited of Oxford and the Historic Towns Trust, the Centre of East Anglian Studies at the University of East Anglia, Terry Slater of Birmingham University and Alan Godfrey Maps of Gateshead. Michael Aston and James Bond kindly gave permission to use six maps from their book *The Landscape of Towns* (Dent, 1976). The map collections of the Departments of Geography at the Universities of Manchester and Salford provided the other map extracts. I am also indebted to Gustav Dobrzynski, cartographer in the Salford department, who drew six new maps as well as redrawing the Aston and Bond maps. Unless otherwise acknowledged, the photographs were taken by the author and prepared from colour slides by Ted Paice of Audio Visual Media, Salford University.

1
Introduction

Urban growth in later medieval England and Wales was startling in its intensity. It was a response to rapidly changing economic conditions and was effected in a variety of ways, giving a hierarchy of towns of different sizes on a variety of sites, each with its own distinctive origins. The result was that, by 1300, most present-day towns were well established.

There are several different ways of looking at this growth, but one of the most interesting is to study how and why the towns grew, not only by investigating the written, cartographic and archaeological records, but also by searching out the surviving medieval features in the town plan.

This book will begin by looking at the nature of medieval towns, why they were needed, how they functioned, and the resultant increase in both their number and their size. Next, the sources of information will be outlined. However, the main part of the book will concentrate on the development of different features in the town plan so that the growth of each town can be described and analysed. Despite the great diversity to be found among these towns, it soon becomes clear that they have many fundamental features in common. Further, it is important to remember that each town changed dramatically in the period under discussion, and we need to reconstruct the complex social and economic processes which were driving the changes in the physical layout of the town.

Armed with a large-scale map, and whatever historical and archaeological evidence can be found, it is usually possible to piece together the history of a town's growth through the medieval period, noting the dates of particular periods of growth, how and why it occurred, and how the layout of the town was altered as a result.

Urban growth

At the time of the Domesday Survey in 1086 there were probably only about fifty places with genuine urban features and functions. Yet by the early fourteenth century the number of towns had reached between five and six hundred, and most had grown considerably in size; such dramatic growth requires some explanation.

At first most urban growth had occurred in places which had been built primarily for defence, but soon it was trade as much as the settlement which required defence. Once established, these early towns acquired other functions, giving them political and perhaps legal status as well. But the take-off in urban growth was powered principally by the great increase in trade during the years of economic growth in the twelfth and, particularly, the thirteenth century.

The old chestnut of 'which came first, towns or trade?' is a classic chicken-and-egg question; the answer is that they are two sides of the same coin, and you could not have one without the other. Throughout the medieval period the increase in trade was sustained by population growth, increasing agricultural production and the emergence of an integrated road and river transport system, all underpinned by lengthy periods of political stability.

Another important reason for the growth of towns lay in the nature of the feudal system which the Normans had imposed. Feudalism placed restrictions on movement and on the ownership of property for the vast majority of the population. Trade needed to be conducted in places immune from these restrictions, and towns were such places. They were non-feudal areas, legally and financially as well as physically separate from the countryside round about, having privileges which allowed the townspeople to own property, as well as to manufacture, buy and sell.

Each town grew up or was established on land which belonged to a feudal landowner, perhaps an abbot, lay seigneur or the king himself. Clearly there was profit to be made from a town, whether from rents on burgage plots and market stalls, from tolls paid by outsiders to use the market, or from fines imposed on those who broke the town's regulations. At the very least a town ought to yield more profit than the arable land which it replaced, and all for very little effort on the part of the seigneur.

Towns never contained more than one in twenty of the population of England and Wales until at least 1700. Moreover, towns with a population of over a thousand were comparatively few in number, and many townspeople continued to have strong rural interests. Nevertheless, the combined importance of the towns was far greater than their population might suggest, simply because most trading, whether of grain, animals or manufactured goods, was conducted in them.

Over half of the towns simply grew from existing settlements, usually by becoming a local market centre, then acquiring a

market charter from the seigneur, and perhaps having this con-
firmed by the king. Some 1200 places obtained royal market
charters between 1227 and 1350, reflecting the enormous growth
in both the national and local trading systems. Yet fewer than
half of these places went on to obtain a full borough charter, the
legal document confirming urban status. The growth of towns in
this fashion has been described as 'organic'.

But other towns were deliberately 'planted' by seigneurs; this
process had been going on in England since the eighth century.
Over 250 new towns were created; two-thirds of them were in
England, and one-third in Wales. The kings themselves established one in eight of the new towns, notably in the earlier years
when it was in their political interest to have strong urban sup-
port. Various ecclesiastics (such as bishops and abbots) established a further three in eight of these towns, and lay seigneurs
the remaining half. Sometimes the particular origins of a town
are reflected in its name, as at Kingston upon Hull, Melcombe
Regis and Bishop's Castle, though not all places with such pro-
prietorial names were newly created. On the other hand, many
new towns have the element 'New' in their name, such as Newcastle, Newport and Newton.

In the thirteenth century alone 65 new towns were established
in England and 46 in Wales; in England the peak was between
1190 and 1230, but in Wales it was in the last three decades of the
century, coinciding with Edward I's military operations against
the Welsh. The vast majority of town plantations were successful;
only one in seven failed, usually because they were poorly situated and failed to attract trade. Many of the most important
towns of the period were new foundations, including Boston,
King's Lynn, Newcastle upon Tyne, Hull, Ludlow and Pontefract. By the end of the fourteenth century the largest new town
was Salisbury (New Sarum), although it is a rather special case,
having been moved from the earlier unsatisfactory site at Old
Sarum in the years around 1220.

The distinction often made between new and organic towns is
not particularly useful in studying their growth. It was once
thought that all new towns had planned layouts, whilst organic
towns just grew. But what seems to have happened in most cases
was that both types of town grew by means of small planned or
unplanned additions; very few had a grand master plan laid out
from the start. New Winchelsea was one of those few; its plan
was ambitiously large, and it was never fully settled. The way in
which most towns grew had very little to do with their origins.

Not all towns grew during the medieval period. (Several suffered relative or even absolute decline;) Thetford, Stamford, Wallingford, Lewes, Wilton and Shaftesbury all lost out, (perhaps because they were no longer in the right place for trade, or because other towns had usurped their positions.) The most spectacular loser was Winchester; as the former royal capital of Wessex it was probably the fourth largest town at the end of the eleventh century, but it progressively lost its administrative functions and had fallen to about fourteenth place by 1334. By then the ten largest towns were probably in this order: 1 London; 2 York; 3 Bristol*; 4 Norwich; 5 Plymouth*; 6 Coventry*; 7 Lincoln; 8 Salisbury*; 9 King's Lynn*; 10 Colchester. The starred towns had risen from lower down the list, and their substantial growth was due to new patterns of commerce and, in most cases, to the availability of navigable water for both internal and overseas trade. Coventry is the obvious exception to this rule, but it lay in the centre of England where no towns had access to navigable rivers.

The creation and growth of towns slowed down in the fourteenth century, reflecting the ceiling which had been reached in most aspects of the economy by about 1310. The Black Death, which arrived in 1348, reduced populations generally by about 40 per cent, and towns were no exception; thereafter most stagnated for well over a century. The last medieval new town seems to have been Queenborough on the Isle of Sheppey, founded in 1368; it never grew beyond a single street. Urban growth effectively ceased until the revival of economic growth under the Tudors in the sixteenth century.

Thus the great period of medieval town growth lasted less than two hundred years, from the mid twelfth to the early fourteenth century. Over half the new towns in England were established between 1150 and 1250, and almost half of all towns have their earliest evidence of urban status in the thirteenth century. In political terms the main period of urban growth coincided with the period between the accession of Henry II and the death of Edward I.

What is a 'medieval town'?
It may seem pedantic to ask such a basic question, but it is important for several reasons. First, we need to be aware that the functions of medieval towns were not identical to those of towns today; second, we need to have criteria to help judge whether a particular place was really a small town, or just a large village

with a market; third, listing the criteria which made a place a town will give some insight into how the town functioned, and what features it possessed.

M. W. Beresford in his classic book *New Towns of the Middle Ages* (1967) suggested that for a place to be a town it should have *one* of these features:

1. Borough charter
2. Burgages (burgage tenure, or the presence of burgesses)
3. Referred to as *burgus* in the assize rolls (or separately represented by a jury before the judge of assize)
4. Taxed as a borough
5. Sent members to any medieval Parliament.

This list has been supplemented in an attempt to establish whether places were towns in Anglo-Saxon times; for medieval towns these additional criteria are useful in adding to Beresford's admittedly legalistic definitions, and they bring us closer to the life of the town itself:

6. Defences
7. Planned street system
8. Market(s)
9. Mint
10. Role as a central place
11. Large or dense population
12. Diversified economic base
13. Social differentiation
14. Complex religious organisation
15. Judicial centre.

None of these latter criteria alone would have made a place a town, but the existence of three or four of them certainly would, whether or not the place was a borough in any legal sense. Some places were given a borough charter before any settlement had begun (in order to attract settlers); if such 'towns' were abortive or decayed after a brief period, they may never have functioned as towns at all. Thus legal definitions alone are unreliable as the sole evidence of urban status. Equally, size alone did not make a place a town; some of the Lincolnshire siltland townships had populations of three to five thousand in the early fourteenth century, but they remained as agricultural communities with no urban attributes.

2
Sources

The study of medieval towns is able to draw on four main groups of source materials: first, the surviving features in the town itself; second, archaeological remains; third, written records; and fourth, maps.

Surviving features

Surviving buildings from medieval times are principally the large structures such as castles, churches and some public buildings, as well as town gates and walls, market places, monastic precincts, bridges and mills. Very few houses survive; most were built in wood and were subject to the ravages of fire and decay. Those which did survive were usually rebuilt in stone around 1600, and the few which were not rebuilt are likely to be atypical, representing the well built houses of the elite, in no way representative of the vast bulk of medieval houses. However, most property boundaries and street layouts seem to have survived intact, often until today, or at least until they were recorded by the large-scale mapping done by the Ordnance Survey in the nineteenth century.

Where medieval structures have been destroyed only since the late nineteenth century or so, there may also be photographic evidence; and by using topographical views and written evidence we may be able to extend our knowledge of the buildings and layout back as far as the sixteenth century.

Archaeological remains

Medieval archaeology is still a relatively new subject, and work in towns is awkward because of the difficulty of access. Buildings are usually standing on sites which would be interesting to excavate, and such sites may not come up for redevelopment for many years. War damage, clearance and rebuilding may also have removed much evidence, as in Coventry. Worse, modern building methods generally involve deep excavation, and the entire archaeological record may already have been removed forever without a full investigation having taken place. Any new development will almost certainly remove the record, and thus 'rescue archaeology' is vital in recording each site, though there may be insufficient time and money to allow a thorough job to

1. Winchester: the excavated site of the Nunnaminster, which occupied a site near the east gate until the eleventh century; it was later replaced by St Mary's Abbey.

be undertaken. Finally, the small size of most urban excavations does tend to present something of a 'keyhole' view of the medieval town.

Despite all these difficulties, much has now been achieved, and archaeological studies can give us much detail of a town's changing structure, functions and occupations. Details have been revealed of castles at Banbury, Bedford and Wallingford, town walls at Shrewsbury and Worcester, roads at Oxford and Winchester, wharves at King's Lynn and London, the cathedral precinct at Wells, and a whole host of ecclesiastical buildings (figure 1). Elsewhere features including bridges, hospitals, water supplies, industrial sites, tenements and gardens have also been revealed. Good summaries are given in books by Martin Carver and John Steane (see 'Further reading'), whilst Colin Platt's *The English Medieval Town* rests on a firm archaeological foundation. Most historic towns now have strategies for future archaeological investigation, based on detailed studies of each town's layout, using all the different sources noted here. Many such studies have been published, particularly since the mid 1970s, and they can provide much useful information. Some were drawn up under the threat of redevelopment; for example, Hull's 1975 strategy was in response to a planned ring road through part of the old town.

Written records

Written records can be a rich source of information, especially for the larger towns, though small towns may have next to nothing. There are four basic types of document. First are literary sources, histories, descriptions, chronicles and annals; a good example is William of Worcester's description of Bristol in the 1470s. Second are the various state records, in particular the Pipe, Patent, Close and Fine Rolls, and the Inquisitions Post Mortem. Third are church and monastic records, which often include wills and inventories. Fourth are the town's own records, which may contain accounts, murage grants, market and borough charters, taxation records and deeds of property. Some towns are fortunate in having records from an early date, though others start disappointingly late.

An introduction to these documents (as well as to the other sources) is given by Palliser (see 'Further reading'). It is impossible to generalise about such a wide variety of records, but perhaps some flavour can be gained from a few of the early written references to Ludlow. The first mention of a town here is in the chronicles of Melsa Abbey, where it is stated that the castle and town were reduced by King Stephen in about 1139. A literary work, the *Fitzwarine Romance,* appears to give some description of the town's layout in the 1140s, and various state and hundred rolls refer to the town and its inhabitants from 1168 onwards. There is a reference to a bridge over the river Teme in a hospital charter of 1220, followed by a series of murage grants from 1233 to 1304; a rental of a local guild dated about 1270 lists the existing streets and names many tenants.

Most documentary sources are accessible, usually in county record offices or in the better local history libraries, though some records may not have been transcribed or published. Worse problems may arise when records are still in private hands; these may not even have been catalogued, and access may be difficult.

Maps

Maps are often ignored or regarded as poor evidence by historians, but there is a rich store of town plans going back into the sixteenth century which can reveal much about urban growth and change. The earliest known is a sketch of Bristol from *c.*1479, and a further dozen towns have maps before the appearance of John Speed's plans in 1612. These are the first standardised plans and were published as insets on his county maps (figure 2). His plan of Gloucester, for example, shows the town walls as they

2. John Speed's plan of Hereford, 1610, shows the extent of suburbs at that date, as well as features such as the castle which have since vanished.

were before the seventeenth-century alterations, and the location of two churches and a bridge which are no longer extant.

After Speed, the number of plans increases steadily, reaching a peak in the first half of the nineteenth century, though some towns (usually the smaller or less prosperous ones) may have no plans at all until quite a late date. Most plans were printed, but manuscript plans were also made, usually depicting the holdings of a particular individual (figure 3). The large-scale county maps of the late eighteenth century often included town plans, and there is a whole series of perspective views ('prospects') of towns. There are also specialised plans showing particular features such as ownership, parish boundaries or individual tenements.

Virtually any old map of a town may yield some detail of the medieval town since lost. Older maps are generally less accurate, and all maps are selective in what they show; they over-emphasise certain features whilst omitting others, although they may show features such as street and house names or parish boundaries which are not always visible on the ground.

The most important single group of maps for our purposes is the large-scale plans done by the Ordnance Survey between 1843 and 1894. They were published at three scales: 1:1056 (5 feet to one mile), 1:528 (10 feet to one mile) and the 'metric ten-foot' scale of 1:500. At such enormous scales the detail shown is immense, with street and property layouts clearly and accurately shown, depicting most towns before any modern large-scale redevelopment. All towns of more than four thousand people were surveyed, almost four hundred towns in all; several extracts from these plans appear later in the book. If these plans were not made for a particular town, there are still those at the 25 inch

3. Thomas Lewis's manuscript plan of Carmarthen, 1786, shows in detail the property of one John Vaughan, though there is no shortage of detail of the rest of the town. (Dyfed Record Office.)

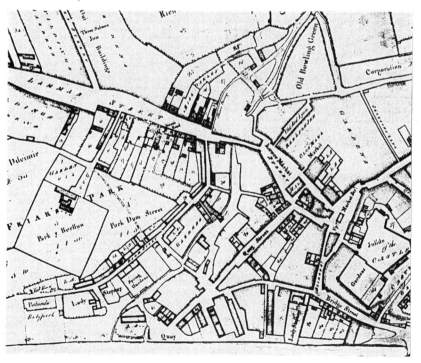

scale (1:2500) which were first surveyed between 1854 and 1893; they still have a great amount of detail, especially if they are enlarged on a modern photocopier. (Do not copy Ordnance Survey maps less than fifty years old — they are copyright!) All these maps depict the towns many centuries after the medieval period, and great care must be exercised in using them; on the other hand the principal features of most towns seem to have changed surprisingly little between medieval times and the nineteenth century. A full description of the great variety of map sources is given by Hindle (see 'Further reading').

Assembling the evidence

The next step is to bring together all the available documentary, archaeological and cartographic evidence and then to set foot in the town to look at the features which are described in the next eight chapters. For although much can be gained from an armchair study, there is no alternative to getting a feel for the town, seeing its site and how the town is laid out upon it, and

4. *Historic Towns* plan of Caernarfon. This map is derived from various maps drawn around 1800 and shows detail of the town as it was in late medieval times. (From Lobel, 1969, by courtesy of Lovell Johns Limited, Oxford, and the Historic Towns Trust.)

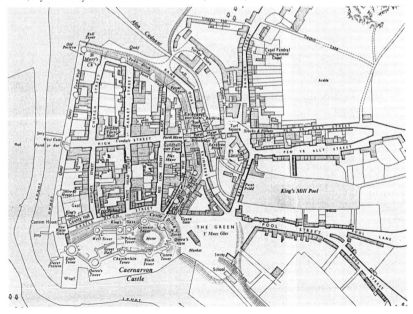

perhaps trying to get into the shoes of the medieval town planner (if such a person ever existed). Many features remain from medieval times, whilst others will have vanished, now recorded only in the historical record or on maps. The trick is to combine all the evidence from the source materials with the features in the town, in order to try to see why, when, where and how each town grew in medieval times.

If a model is needed, then probably one of the best is Lobel's series *Historic Towns,* which deals with Banbury, Caernarfon, Glasgow, Gloucester, Hereford, Nottingham, Reading and Salisbury in volume 1, and Bristol, Cambridge, Coventry and Norwich in volume 2 and London in volume 3 (figure 4). In these studies the historical record for each town is combined with evidence from early large-scale town plans to produce both a description and a map of the medieval town.

3
Site

The location of a town is of great importance in understanding its layout and growth. Successful organic towns prospered because they were in the right situation for trade with regard to roads or navigable water, even if the actual site sometimes presented problems for the town.

On the other hand, the creators of new towns were able to exercise some choice in locating their settlements. There was usually little problem in obtaining a site; only a small area was needed, and the landowner simply had to choose the right spot. It was difficult to move a town later if the wrong choice had been made. New towns were usually situated in a corner of an existing parish, and they could easily be made into a parish in their own right in due course. Sometimes the site of a new town was not deliberately chosen at all; where a new castle or abbey was being built, then a settlement would almost certainly grow outside its gates, peopled by those engaged in building, by those providing services and trade, and by others seeking protection (figure 5).

But what ensured a town's success was a combination of its geographical position and the commercial acumen of its townsfolk. If a town was to prosper in the longer term, it had to be on

5. Ludlow: the early settlement of Dinham probably grew immediately outside the gate of the castle keep but was destroyed when the outer bailey was built.

6. Exeter: remains of the medieval bridge over the river Exe, which was surmounted by a chapel. The town was originally established by the Romans at this lowest crossing point of the river.

important trade routes; there are numerous examples of towns failing because they were only a short distance from a main road (figure 9). Beresford sums up the matter thus: 'planting a town was different from planting a hedge. A hedge might grow anywhere, but a town's fortunes were not independent of its geographical position.'

Ultimately, then, trade was the reason for urban growth. In England three-quarters of the larger towns had access to navigable water, whether river or sea, and some seigneurs spent money to improve navigations or build wharves. Thus a good site for a town was on an important road or at a road junction; being situated on a navigable river or at a bridging point as well was even better, though the most prosperous towns were also seaports (figure 6). In some cases new roads were built to towns which had been sited away from roads for other reasons; Hull was well placed for river trading, but in the early days few roads led to it. In other cases roads were diverted or bridges built to bring traffic into or through a town, as at Bridgnorth and Appleby. In Ludlow a new bridge succeeded in diverting traffic up the new Broad Street, thus taking it through the town's large market place, rather than passing by one end of it (figure 36).

Roads had strategic importance, especially in the Welsh Marches; towns in this border region were primarily defensive in nature, and often declined in times of peace. A further difficulty arose where towns had been placed on a very defensive site for military reasons; they might find themselves very poorly placed for trade. Such sites were often used for new towns in the early days of the Norman Conquest and continued to be used in and around Wales until the end of the thirteenth century.

The smaller physical details of the site were not unimportant, simply because it was far more difficult in those days to correct or improve an inadequate site than it would be today. Beresford says that 'some sites were the triumph of optimism over harsh physical obstacles' whilst other towns in 'text-book situations could end with grass growing in their market places'. The reasons for the choice of a site are rarely well documented; clearly there were basic requirements such as a prominent position, reasonably flat land (unless defence was important), a good water supply and the avoidance of marshes (figure 10).

Some towns grew on the site of Roman towns, others enlarged on Anglo-Saxon or Danish foundations, others grew or were made from existing villages, whilst yet others were planted on what might be thought to have been 'green-field sites'. However, no town was planted or grew on a virgin site; there were always some features present in the landscape, and the town would have to adjust to them. Pre-existing features might include roads, field patterns and boundaries, houses, churches, castles, old defensive works and street systems; any of these would influence the choice of site or the development of a town's internal layout. It is not easy to try to envisage what the site was like before urban growth, but long-vanished features may have played an important role in the development of the town plan.

Once established, the town would have very definitive geographical limits, even if it was not walled. It was important that villeins living outside the town did not share its privileges and liberties, although they might not be jealous of the town's higher rate of tax. If the town acquired its own legal jurisdiction, then it was also important to know how far the authority of its courts extended. Thus a town's boundaries were well known, documented and sometimes perambulated. The bounds of some Welsh boroughs are very large; Conwy's measure some 30 km (18 miles). At the other extreme, most English planted towns covered only a few acres; Boroughbridge was 40 ha (95 acres) and Bishop's Castle only 5 ha (11 acres).

4
Plan layouts

The next step in looking at a medieval town plan is to make an assessment of its overall layout. The disposition of the streets is the principal feature, to which must be added the defences (if any), market, churches and property boundaries, in order to try to separate different areas which have common plan features. Small towns may have only one such *plan unit*, but most towns have several, representing different periods of growth. Even apparently simple layouts may conceal a complex history. M. R. G. Conzen was the first to try to define such units in British towns, with studies of Alnwick, Newcastle, Conwy and Ludlow (see 'Further reading'). The method relies on the basic premise that most features of the town plan, in particular streets and property boundaries, are remarkably permanent features, and that any major changes since medieval times will probably have been recorded, or will themselves be obvious in the town's layout. Such studies may also reveal periods of urban growth which are unclear or absent from the documentary record.

Allowing for the fact that some towns will not fit into any classification, there are five general types of town layout (many of the examples used are taken from Aston and Bond's *The Landscape of Towns*).

Towns with central open market places
Many older organic towns have this layout, including abbey towns and some which grew outside the gates of a castle. Typically the market place is triangular in shape, usually because the market developed at the junction of three roads; others are rectangular or irregular. Examples include St Albans, Market Harborough, Bampton (Oxfordshire), Taunton, Richmond (North Yorkshire) and Alnwick (figures 7 and 25).

Linear towns
Linear towns are very common, frequently occurring where a town grew along a road. Such towns often consisted of little more than a single row of house plots on each side of the road, which was sometimes widened to accommodate a market area. These towns were nearly always undefended and became much commoner from the mid twelfth century, when there was little need

for defence. Typical examples include Henley-in-Arden and Chipping Campden. Where towns were added to an existing settlement, the layout adopted was also often a single street, laid out at some distance from the church and manor house of the earlier settlement; this occurred at Marshfield and Wickwar.

The growing importance of roads and the trade which they brought is demonstrated by the number of places where roads were diverted into new or growing towns; this happened at Thame, Dunster, Montacute and Chipping Sodbury. Indeed, older settlements which lay a little way from an important road might be left high and dry as urban development became concentrated along the road; this can be seen at Brackley, Chard and Brough. In this last case an attempt was made to plant a town outside the new castle, and a church was founded nearby; but the main road descending from Stainmore passed by 550 metres (600 yards) to the north, and the market town grew there instead (figure 9).

Castle towns

Many towns developed or were planted outside the gates of a castle; the commonest layout was a single street running from the castle with house plots on each side, enclosed by a ditch or wall which was often effectively an outer bailey for the castle (figure 4). There are numerous examples of such layouts in Wales and the Marches, though many failed to survive as trading towns once defence ceased to be important. Richard's Castle had over one hundred burgages in 1304; its motte-and-bailey castle and church still survive, but little else remains of the town. Other examples include Kilpeck, Whitecastle, Skenfrith and Bere. Many castle towns did survive, sometimes by completely altering their layout; Kidwelly and Denbigh relocated their markets and town centres outside the castle walls which had formerly enclosed them (figure 8). Many other towns have had their layouts strongly influenced by a castle, even if the towns themselves were not defended. Broad market places grew up outside the castle gates at Windsor, Skipton and Taunton, whilst towns such as Launceston, Wisbech, Pleshey, Tutbury and Richmond (North Yorkshire) were all influenced by their castles (figure 25). Devizes is a rather curious example where a town grew around the castle's large outer bailey and then expanded into the bailey when it was no longer needed.

Rectilinear plans

It used to be thought that most new towns planted in England and Wales were laid out on a grid plan, and Ludlow, Salisbury

7. Bampton, Oxford-shire: the triangular market place. Such markets often formed at the junction of three roads; there has been some infilling of the market area. (After M. Aston and J. Bond, *The Landscape of Towns,* Dent, 1976.)

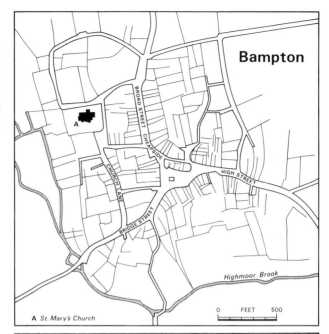

A *St. Mary's Church*

8. Denbigh: the former walled town and new market site. The town moved from the con-fined outer bailey of the castle to a more spa-cious site outside. (After M. Aston and J. Bond, *The Landscape of Towns,* Dent, 1976.)

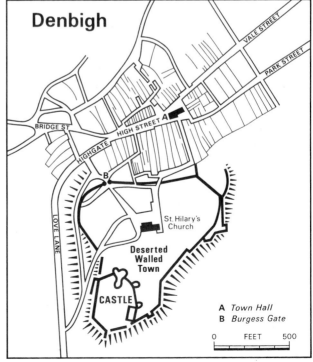

A *Town Hall*
B *Burgess Gate*

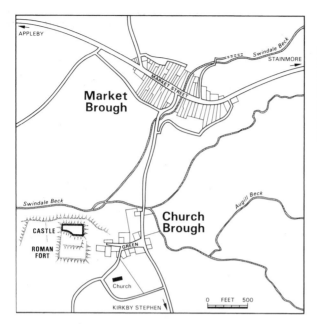

9. Brough: linear market town and failed earlier centre. The plantation at Church Brough failed to prosper, and urban growth took place on the road descending from Stainmore.

and New Winchelsea were presented as examples. The problem was that no one defined what constituted a grid; a possible definition might be that a grid plan should have been conceived and laid out in a single operation and be made up of two sets of parallel roads of similar width (and thus importance), dividing the town into a number of blocks or chequers; the roads need not all be exactly parallel, nor need they cross at right angles. The crucial question is then what is the minimum number of chequers needed to make a grid? The answer is perhaps between nine and twelve; anything less can hardly be described as a grid and should simply be called rectilinear. A few right-angled street junctions do not constitute a grid. On this basis there are only a handful of medieval grid-pattern towns, and the best are at New Winchelsea and Salisbury (figures 10 and 12). Ludlow is not a grid at all but has three parallel streets (laid out at different dates) connected and separated by narrow back and cross lanes (see chapter 11).

Rectilinear street layouts, however, are reasonably common, especially if a new area of the town was being established; straight roads and right angles made laying out the plots much easier. Examples include Stratford-upon-Avon, Newport (Dyfed), New Radnor, Shipston on Stour, Caernarfon, Flint and many other Welsh planted towns (figures 4 and 11). Some rectilinear plans are not medieval in origin at all but are based on earlier street layouts. Roman plans have influenced the layout of

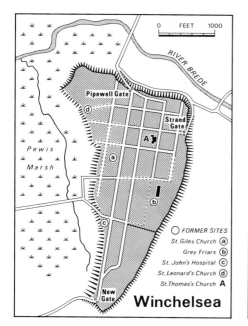

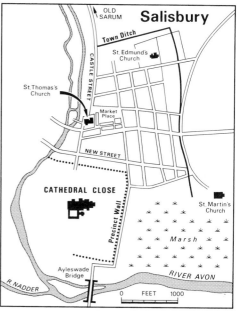

10. New Winchelsea and Salisbury: grid-plan towns. Two rare examples of large-scale formal town planning; Winchelsea was founded in 1283, and Salisbury *c*.1220. (After M. Aston and J. Bond, *The Landscape of Towns*, Dent, 1976.)

11. Shipston on Stour: rectilinear plan. A classic example of a town being enlarged in stages; this is clearly not a grid plan. The market has been partly infilled. (After M. Aston and J. Bond, *The Landscape of Towns*, Dent, 1976.)

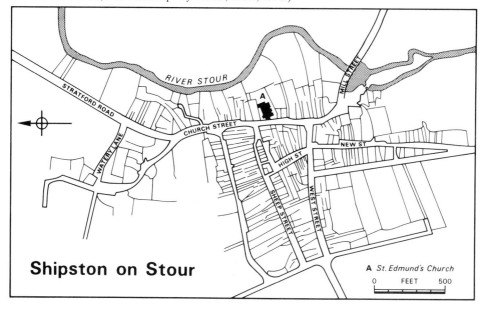

Dorchester, Exeter, Colchester, Bath and Winchester, though the correspondence is not always exact; Anglo-Saxon rectilinear planning is evident at Wareham, Cricklade, Wallingford and Oxford.

Composite plans

Many town plans do not fit into any one of the first four categories simply because they have been subject to planned or unplanned growth occurring in different ways at different dates. The old idea of planted towns having planned layouts, and organic towns somehow evolving of their own accord is clearly untrue. Many planned towns have an organic core which represents an earlier settlement or the early stages of market growth before any formal layout of burgages was undertaken. Few towns had a grand master plan; most were added to over a long period for many different reasons and now contain areas which were

12. Salisbury: each of the chequers of the town's grid plan had a name; this twin-gabled house bears the name 'Three Lyon Chequer'.

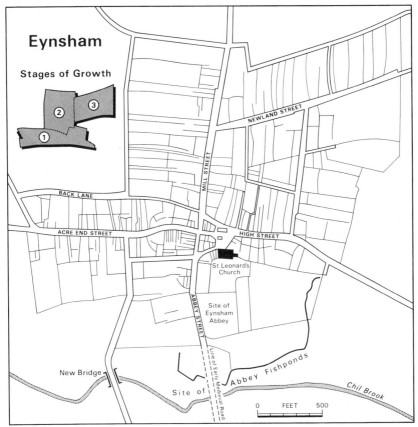

13. Eynsham: composite layout. The three phases of growth are indicated; the Newland Street unit can be dated precisely at 1215, when there was a charter for a borough extension. (After M. Aston and J. Bond, *The Landscape of Towns,* Dent, 1976).

consciously planned alongside unplanned piecemeal additions (figure 13). Some towns even have distinct areas which developed independently; in Coventry the Prior's half of the town grew around a triangular market place, whilst the Earl's half developed along the High Street.

Investigating the overall layout of a town is only the first step in studying the medieval town plan; we need to look at each of the plan features in turn before we can begin to see how the town grew. As so much of this chapter has been concerned with the streets it seems logical to continue by looking at them in more detail.

14. Ludlow: Broad Street is a typical wide medieval street (it reaches 23 metres, 75 feet, in width); the trading of cattle and grain may well have overflowed here from the main market square.

15. Ludlow: Raven Lane (Le Narrow Lane) lies between Broad Street and Mill Street; it is clearly a back lane, not in any way equal to the wide main streets of the town, although it may have had a few poor burgages.

5

Streets

The streets are the most obvious large-scale surviving feature of the medieval town. Most towns have some streets which were formally planned, as well as others which were created or extended without any formal control as demand for space increased. All new streets, whether planned or unplanned, would have had to adjust to pre-existing features in the landscape, such as field systems and boundaries, tenements, paths or lanes, as well as physical obstacles such as steep slopes or marshy areas.

Most medieval streets were quite spacious; the main streets were used as markets and therefore had to be wide, especially if the cattle trade was important. In Ludlow, Broad Street certainly lived up to its name (figures 14, 20 and 36). The charters of some later planned towns specified the widths of the streets; those at Stratford-upon-Avon were to be 50 feet (15 metres) wide, and this was by no means an unusual width. Thus the notion of all medieval streets being narrow alleyways is not true. Indeed, some narrow streets were only created by late or post-medieval infilling of market places (see chapter 7). Narrow alleyways did exist, some leading to courtyards, others weaving their way through the burgage plots, giving access to the rear of properties or simply providing a way through from one street to the next (figure 16). Where burgage plots ran in a long uninterrupted series, back lanes would usually provide rear access, and cross-lanes might run through the series, all forming an integral part of the street plan (figure 15).

In most towns the street pattern, once established, was rarely changed, but there are exceptions. Streets were diverted or stopped up for a variety of reasons; a main road might have been deliberately shifted so as to pass through the town centre, a new bridge built in a different place to the old bridge or ford which it replaced, or a castle or monastic precinct enlarged over part of the town (figures 13, 17 and 36).

In particular, the relationship between the streets and the town wall can be complicated. It is important to establish which came first in each part of the town in order to understand which would tend to control the other. Thus, if the wall preceded urban development, the streets would usually be extended up to the wall, perhaps with streets parallel to the wall (inside or out), the

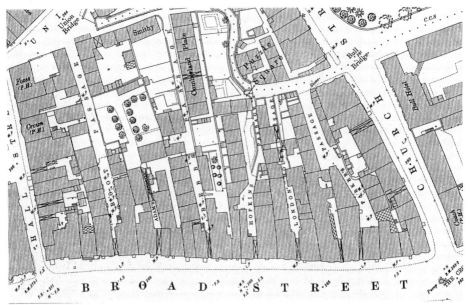

16. Welshpool: burgage plots and alleyways. The Ordnance Survey 1:500 plan of 1885 clearly shows the burgage plots, and the alleyways leading through to the rear tenements.

17. Ludlow: Christ Croft. The Ordnance Survey 1:500 plan (1885) shows this former ditch/ street in Dinham, probably the oldest part of the town.

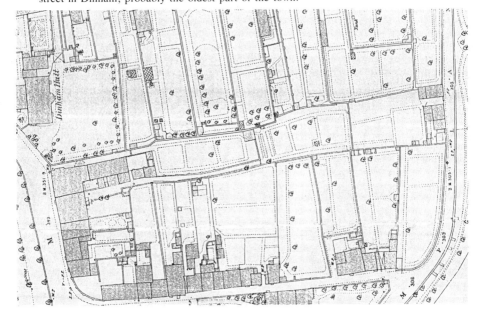

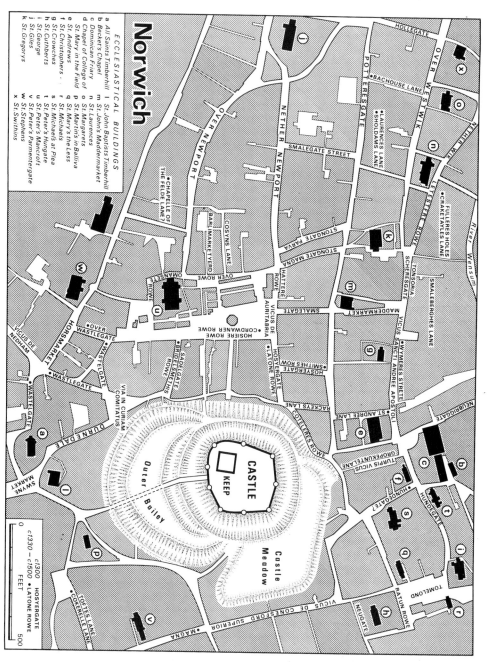

18. Norwich: medieval street names, rows, markets and churches. This is the crowded centre of the town, with the main market square outside St Peter Mancroft.

wall and streets fitting neatly together (figure 21). If, on the other
hand, a wall was built around or through an existing area of the
town, the whole layout might look less coherent, especially if the
wall had cut through part of the existing townscape.

Street names can provide much useful evidence about the
status of streets and about the trades carried on. It is important to
ascertain the names in use in medieval times, for they do not
always pass down the centuries unchanged. Finding out these
names from the written record can be difficult, and it is not
always clear to which street a particular name refers. Rentals can
be very useful sources of information, and studies such as those
by the English Place Name Society can also be a great help.

In Coventry, Frerelane led to the Franciscan friary, the High
Street was called just that (*Altus Vicus*), and from it Erles-
mullane (Earls's Mill Lane) led to Newstret. The elements 'New'
and 'Old' can be especially useful in helping to establish the chronology of town growth and may also indicate street diversions. In
Ludlow, Old Street is the route traffic used to take through the
town before the new bridge was built (figure 36). Norwich had
market streets called Vicus de Swyne Market and Horsmarket,
trading streets such as Potteresgate and Fischeregate, and individual rows of shops near the market such as Hosiere Rowe and
Coteleres Rowe. On a less respectable front, the records here
also reveal Hor Lane and Gropekuntelane (figure 18)!

In Winchester there were five specialist street names as early
as AD 1000; they were named after tanners, shield-makers, butchers, goldsmiths and shoemakers. Four of these are concerned
with noisome animal products, and this shows that such trades
were concentrated in particular areas from an early date. The
names are not always a reliable indication of activity; no Winchester shoemakers lived in their street (Scowrtenestret) in 1148,
and it was later called Jewry Street. Rather curiously, the butchers' street (Flesmangerestret) moved its location sometime
between 1100 and 1300.

Many street names live on long after the features they describe
have disappeared. An interesting example occurs in Hereford
where the narrow West Street/East Street (formerly Packers
Lane) runs across the centre of the town. In medieval times it was
called Behyndethewall Lane, but there was no wall in front of it;
this was already an old name then, referring to the earlier Saxon
wall which had been demolished when the town grew beyond it
in the eleventh century.

6
Defences

Castles

Castles were, as we have seen, often the *raison d'être* for a town. Eighteen of the first 25 planted towns after the Conquest were alongside castles, and the proportion of towns growing outside castles in Wales and the Marches remained very high throughout the medieval period. Overall, 30 per cent of English new towns were alongside castles, whilst the figure for Wales was 85 per cent.

The castle was very much a Norman introduction to England; many places had been defended by ditches and palisades before 1066, but there were only a handful of castles before that date. The first castles were of the motte-and-bailey design, but the most important ones were soon surmounted by stone keeps and ultimately were replaced by full-blown medieval castles with their massive walls and gates. Some castles were enlarged several times, and it is important to establish the chronology of enlargement, for this might have had important consequences for the town plan. Some castles were built or enlarged over areas of the existing town, requiring demolition of houses and the loss of tenements; this happened in towns such as Winchester, Norwich, Oxford, Colchester and Shrewsbury. In the early years of the Conquest, 166 houses were demolished in Lincoln (figure 28), and fifty tenements (one-fifth of the town) were lost at Shrewsbury.

In Wales and its Marches some towns grew entirely within the protection of the outer bailey of the castle, whilst many town walls effectively formed an extension to the defensive system of the castle (figures 4 and 8). But towns became increasingly independent of castles as the need for defence declined. We have already noted the new undefended town centres at Kidwelly and Denbigh, and the growth of Devizes into the former outer bailey of the castle.

A few castles have disappeared, principally the early motte-and-bailey constructions which were never rebuilt in stone. A contrasting pair which contradicts this rule can be seen in the Welsh borders; at Richard's Castle the earth motte-and-bailey survives largely intact, whilst at Bishop's Castle, where the castle was rebuilt in stone, only a stunted mound now remains,

19. York: Bootham Bar. York's walls were mainly built on Roman and Danish foundations, but by medieval times their main purpose was symbolic rather than defensive.

surmounted by a bowling-green. Rather curiously, though, the town of Richard's Castle has disappeared, whilst that at Bishop's Castle survives.

Town defences

Town defences range from a single gate through to a complete circuit of walls, with or without a castle. Defences of some sort were built at over a quarter of medieval towns, though virtually all Welsh new towns were defended. Some towns utilised, maintained, improved and even enlarged the circuits of Roman, Saxon or Danish lines of defence, whilst others constructed entirely new walls (figure 19). Many defences began as a simple ditch and bank which might later be surmounted by a wooden palisade; at towns such as Cambridge, Lichfield, St Albans and Salisbury the defences never progressed beyond this stage (figure 10). More often such early works were replaced by a stone wall with gates to control access. Walls were nearly always connected to the castle, if there was one. A few towns had fortified bridges; the only ones which survive are at Monmouth and Warkworth, though they formerly existed in several towns, including Bedford, Oxford, Bridgnorth and Durham.

The reasons for the building of town walls are not always obvious; clearly in some areas and at particular periods there was a real need for defence from attack or for the defence of trade. Fear, in times of internal disruption, was also important; such periods included the reigns of Stephen and Matilda, and of King John, as well as the baronial revolts of the 1260s and the invasion scares of the fourteenth century. Royal boroughs tended to be walled, whilst those controlled by the church did not. Most English towns did not have defences, especially the lesser towns of the Midlands and south-east. And most of those towns which did acquire town walls did not do so until the thirteenth century, having grown for centuries without them.

Most towns did not need defensive walls, and in any case few walls could withstand a serious attack; Berwick's substantial defences were overrun by the Scots in 1318. There was no good defensive reason for a town in the middle of England like Coventry to begin building its walls in the early fourteenth century, especially when they were not completed until two centuries later.

Many town walls were built or improved to demonstrate the political importance and independence of the town; walls were something which no self-respecting town could be without. Thus most town walls were civic status symbols rather than defensive structures, and some towns incorporated depictions of gates in their civic crests. In some places houses were built into the walls, and chapels into gates (figure 30). Gates helped to control access into the town and were convenient places where tolls could be charged. A few towns, unable to afford to build or complete their walls, simply built gates across the main roads; this happened at Chesterfield, Henley-in-Arden and Tewkesbury. If we look back to the list of the ten largest towns in the fourteenth century, they all had defences, whether Roman or medieval in date (or both), some of stone, others of earth.

Wall construction began in earnest in the thirteenth century, the large amount of money needed usually being raised by a murage grant which enabled taxes or tolls to be levied specifically for a town wall. Occasionally, however, although a grant was allowed and money perhaps raised, there is no evidence of any ditch or wall being started; this appears to have happened at Clun in 1277 and at Crickhowell in 1281. On the other hand, many town walls at places as diverse as Pembroke, Warkworth, Boston and Flint were built without any murage grants. Completion of a town's walls commonly took over fifty years, and clearly this was a major undertaking for any town.

The line of a town wall would be controlled by many factors; it would tend to follow the line of any earlier defences and would also be controlled by the pre-existing layout of the town. It might

20. Ludlow: Broad Gate and Broad Street. The street clearly existed before the gate was inserted; also evident are the regular burgage plots of Broad Street, as well as the narrow back and cross lanes.

21. Southampton: The Ordnance Survey 1:500 plan of 1870 shows roads parallel to the town walls, the position of the town ditch, and much other detail.

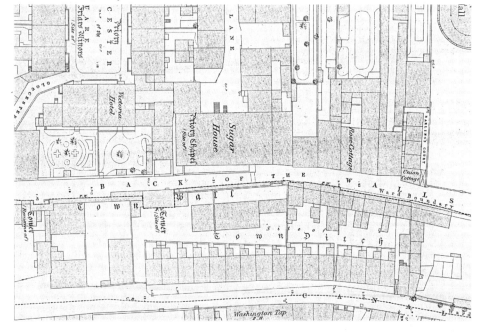

22. Ludlow: Broad Gate is a massive structure which was inserted into the already existing Broad Street by about 1300, perhaps sixty years after the town walls were begun.

aim simply to surround the town, or it might leave some room for expansion, as at Norwich. On the other hand, some walls cut through the existing town, perhaps to take advantage of a break of slope, because they had to follow the town boundary which had not been respected by the populace, or because the town could not afford to enclose the whole built-up area. The massive Broad Gate at Ludlow was clearly inserted into the middle of Broad Street; the pattern of the burgage plots and street frontages runs through the gate as if it were not there (figures 20 and 22).

Once built, the walls clearly delimited the town and controlled its growth. If space within the walls ran out, then further development would have to be extramural. A few towns, such as Bristol and Carmarthen, even enlarged their circuit of walls. Carmarthen's defences have a complicated history; the Roman fort was not reused, but a new castle and town were planted overlooking the river. The first town walls were the subject of the earliest Welsh murage grant in 1233, but the town grew so much that an enlarged circuit was begun in 1415.

The most impressive remaining walls and gates include those at Caernarfon, Chepstow, Conwy, Chester, Denbigh, Newcastle, Norwich, Southampton, Tenby, Yarmouth and York (figures 23 and 24). At the other extreme, some well documented walls, such as those at Haverfordwest, have vanished entirely and have proved well nigh impossible to trace.

Many lengths of wall and gates have been pulled down to make

23. (Above) Chepstow: the 'port walls' were built in the 1270s; they are 2 metres (7 feet) thick, up to 6 metres (20 feet) high, and run for 1.1 km (1200 yards) around the town, enclosing an area of over 45 ha (110 acres).

24. (Right) Caernarfon: the town walls were built at the end of the thirteenth century as part of the overall defensive scheme of the castle and town. The town was planted by Edward I as part of his campaign against the Welsh. (Photograph: Cadbury Lamb.)

way for new roads or to improve access. Where the original walls do not survive intact their course can often be traced on old maps, in documentary references or in the present-day layout of the town. The street layout often indicates the line of lost walls; features include dead-ends (where streets formerly stopped at the wall), roads which used to run around the wall (inside or out), roads built on top of a demolished wall, roads fanning out from long-vanished gates, or streets narrowing where a gate used to be (figures 21 and 31). The layout of property, parish and town boundaries also needs to be inspected, and even street and house names may be of help.

7

Markets

If a medieval town was to continue to grow and flourish, then trade was the key; thus the market areas within the town were uniquely important. Markets originated in villages, in the fortified burhs and planted towns, at cross-roads, outside castle gates or even in churchyards, though they were banned from this last location in 1285. Some towns owe their entire origin to trade, and their market places would usually be at the centre of the town. The market might be stretched out in a cigar shape along a road through the town, or be a more compact shape if it was based on a road junction. Triangular markets were likely to emerge where three roads met, and a rectangular market at the junction of four roads or if the town had a rectilinear street plan. Much has been written on the different shapes of markets, even to the extent of suggesting that the shape of the market would determine the overall layout of the town, but markets come in all shapes and sizes, and size was always more important than shape (figures 7, 18, 26, 31 and 36).

Medieval markets needed to be large in order to accommodate trading in livestock and grain; only the entrances needed to be narrow to control entry and to facilitate the collection of tolls. Stratford-upon-Avon's newly laid-out market was 90 feet (27.5 metres) wide, and that at St Ives (Cambridgeshire) was 120 feet (36.5 metres) in width. Most markets would, originally at least, be a large open space dedicated to trading (figure 25).

Eventually the market might begin to be infilled, especially if cattle trading (which required a large space) was moved out of the town centre. Two processes operated; first, shop fronts might gradually encroach on to the market in order to gain more selling space; and second, stalls set up in the market might become permanent structures (figure 27). It is even possible that some infilling was deliberately planned at an early date in order to increase the income from rents. Unfortunately the process went on largely undocumented, though at Cirencester the townspeople complained in 1343 that the abbots had encroached on the king's highway since 1203 and built houses on the market place. Virtually every market has been infilled to some extent, and the process has continued through to the present day. In larger towns buildings such as market halls, guildhalls or chapels might be

25. Richmond (North Yorkshire): the large semicircular market place grew up outside the castle gates in the early twelfth century; Trinity church was established there before 1135.

built in the market place; most had at least stocks and a market cross. By studying early maps and carefully examining street lines and property boundaries, it should be possible to gauge the original extent of each market (figures 7, 8, 10, 11, 13, 26 and 31).

Some markets were moved during the medieval period, usually in response to the need for more space. At Pontefract the old enclosed borough proved too small and the extramural market of Westcheap was established (figure 31). Other places where deliberate decisions seem to have been taken to move the market were at Bury St Edmunds, Denbigh, Kidwelly and Peterborough. A few towns such as Oxford and Winchester had no special market areas, and here the streets themselves became the markets.

In the medieval town there was rarely any distinction between residential, commercial and industrial districts. All activities were carried on together; artisan workshops were to be found everywhere, with manufacturing, selling and living all in the same premises. Thus virtually every street had some sort of market or trading function. It is hardly surprising to find that certain streets or areas specialised in particular activities or trades or in selling particular commodities; the larger the town, the greater such specialisation became, even at an early date. We have already seen how this is reflected in street names (chapter 5; figure 18), and personal surnames can be equally useful, especially if it is known where the individuals lived.

In Norwich a 26-year series of property deeds has been analysed by Kelly (see 'Further reading') for the years around 1300; many indicate the occupation carried on in the premises. The top fifteen occupations (in order) were: ecclesiastics, merchants, drapers, shoemakers, metalworkers (30 per cent of whom were goldsmiths), tanners, bakers, fishers, dyers, skinners, butchers, tailors, masons, glovers and weavers. This list exaggerates the number of traders who needed a water supply, as that fact would nearly always be mentioned in the deeds. Perhaps the biggest surprise in the list is that there are so few weavers, but by this date weaving had become a much more rural industry, having moved towards the sites of fulling mills outside the towns. Within the town, four of the occupations were remarkably concentrated; most of the tanners worked in only three of the city's eleven districts (sub-leets), on sites with small streams flowing down to the river. Half the dyers were in one sub-leet (also near water supplies), and most of the glovers (who needed to be near butchers) were in another. Finally, half of the metalworkers (principally the goldsmiths and cutlers) were in the two wealthiest sub-leets.

26. Ludlow: market infill. The central part of the market has been partly filled by three rows of shops. Also visible is the market burgage series, with Broad Street and Mill Street leading off to the south.

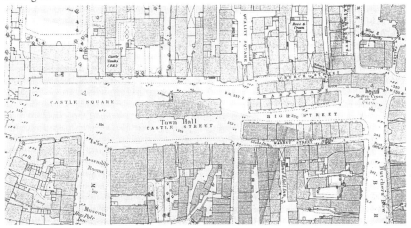

27. Ludlow: the main open market area was established outside the gates of the outer bailey, along the ridge towards the parish church. It was later much infilled (see figure 26), though the prominent market hall has been demolished. (Photograph: Cadbury Lamb.)

Another reason for certain trades being close together was that no one else wanted to live near them; this applied to noxious and noisome trades like butchers, tanners and fishmongers, who were thus often banished to particular quarters or even encouraged to live outside the town, where they might offend people least. The butchers' street or meat market often became known as the Shambles, though this name derives from 'shammels', meaning market stalls. Any trades which required fires to be constantly alight, for example bakers, smiths or potters, were also shunned, as other burgesses wished to minimise the possibility of having their houses burnt down.

Jews also tended to live together, not just because they specialised in particular trades (gold and money-lending), but for reasons of safety and sometimes enforcement. They had begun to arrive in the mid twelfth century, and soon Jewries were established in many towns; the largest were in London, York and Lincoln. Several London parishes had so many Jews that three attached the word 'Jewry' to their name. Even remote Hereford had a Jews Street. Jews were expelled from England in 1290.

The commonest industrial building, the watermill, was rarely seen in towns because it needed a site with good water power, which did not often occur within the bounds of a town. There were four or five mills at Cirencester, though none lay within the town boundary. Winchester, on the other hand, had four mills inside its walls in 1148, and a further six just outside. Thus mills for grinding corn or fulling cloth would never be far away, providing the town with their services.

The numerous towns which were situated on navigable water must have had wharves and other waterfront structures to deal with the transhipment of goods; apart from archaeological work in large ports like London and York, very little is known of this important aspect of medieval trade.

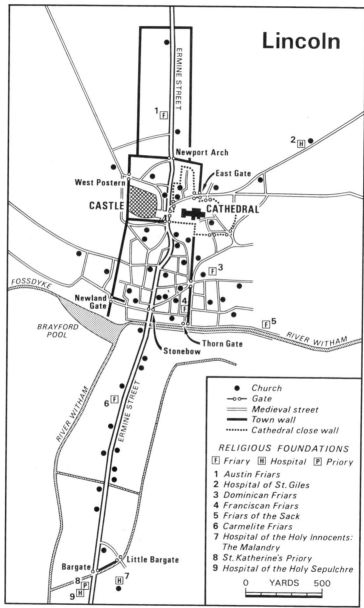

28. Lincoln: churches, friaries and hospitals. The walls, gates and suburbs of this prosperous town can also be seen.

8

Churches

The parish church was usually the major public building in the medieval town, and often the only one built in stone. Where a town had developed from a village, the church normally marks the original nucleus of the settlement (figure 31). The church is usually located in a prominent position, perhaps on high ground, near the market or on an ancient religious site. In planted towns the situation can be much more complex; new towns were founded in existing parishes (often at the edge of them), and obviously the townspeople would soon wish to have their own parish and church. The separation of the town from its old parish and the creation of a new parish required action by the bishop which was not always forthcoming; often only a subsidiary chapel of ease was provided. Some smaller towns never obtained their own parish, and the townsfolk had to walk to the existing church some distance away. Other new towns had full parochial status granted to them at an early date, whilst yet others were fortunate enough to find a church already standing on their site.

Once established, the site of the church was seldom changed, even if there was substantial rebuilding. The chronology of the building and enlargement of the church can usually be ascertained in some detail from the writings of architectural historians, and every substantial alteration can usually be dated reasonably accurately. Pevsner's 'The Buildings of England' series will provide basic data, and many churches have their own published histories.

In general, churches were enlarged in times of prosperity, when the town would be growing too. Excess money in the community, derived from trade, was the force behind these changes, and in an age more pious than our own it was natural to spend money on church building. Thus churches are an excellent barometer of a town's prosperity and growth. The main exception to this is that a few churches were enlarged by the local seigneur as funerary monuments. A few towns did not grow but remained poor; their churches may hardly have been enlarged at all.

Most towns had a single parish church, but there are many exceptions to this rule; London had 97 parishes, Norwich 56, York 39 and Lincoln 34, all within their walls (figures 18, 28 and 29). Winchester had at least 35 inside its walls and about twenty without (figure 30). On the other hand, some large towns, such as Boston or Grantham, never had more than one. The reason for this discrepancy usually lies in the age of the town; before the church reforms of the eleventh century churches belonged to individuals, and any person of wealth and status might establish a church, however small. Thus older towns with many landowners might have numerous tiny churches and private chapels. Clearly many of these parishes were very small, some less than 2 ha (5 acres). Towns founded (or which grew) at a later date usually have only one parish church.

If a town with only one church did grow substantially, then second or even third churches might occasionally be granted, though this required the parish boundaries to be redrawn, with a consequent loss of parishioners (and hence wealth) to the original church or churches. The new town of Salisbury found one church already existing close by; a new town church was established in the market place, probably as a chapel of ease in the first instance. The town grew so much that a third church was added within fifty years, and the parish boundaries were

29. Norwich: the church of St Edmund was probably established before the Norman Conquest and was one of Norwich's total of 56 medieval churches; it is now no longer in use.

30. Winchester: the medieval walls follow the line of the Roman walls; Kingsgate incorporates St Swithun's church on the first-floor level.

redrawn so that there were three equally sized parishes (figure 10).

The pattern of parish boundaries varies enormously from one parish to the next. Organic towns tended to have large parishes, extending far out into the countryside, whereas new towns (usually cut out of existing parishes) were often entirely urban; Okehampton covers only 4 ha (10 acres) out of a mother parish of nearly 4000 ha (10,000 acres). Early town parish boundaries tend to follow natural features or roads, whilst later ones follow property boundaries and streets. Fortunately these boundaries are usually well recorded, they tend to remain unchanged for long periods and can easily be traced in the cartographic record, in particular on the tithe maps drawn in the years around 1840.

Other religious institutions, principally hospitals and monasteries, were of great local importance, and the study of their development can be fundamental to understanding a town's development (figure 28). Hospitals were not only for the old and sick; their name derives from the latin *hospes* (a stranger or guest), and thus they also provided hospitality for travellers, the poor and for that much feared group, lepers. They were often founded by the burgesses as acts of piety and became very numerous; there were probably over a thousand in England alone in the thirteenth century, and no sizable town was without one. St Leonard's Hospital in York had a staff of 26 (half of whom were chaplains), as well as numerous lay helpers, to look after two hundred inmates.

Leper hospitals were often built at the very edge of the town or in the suburbs, and their location can give a clue as to how far the town extended at the date of their foundation. Leprosy became less of a scourge in later medieval times, and the number of leper hospitals declined; their place was increasingly taken by almshouses during the fifteenth century.

The earliest monasteries to be established in towns were able to create monastic precincts for themselves in the town centre; all pre-Conquest houses were Benedictine, and many were in towns. After about 1100 there was an influx of new orders, and some of these (notably the Augustinians) also settled in the towns. Some towns, such as Dunstable, were largely controlled by the monks.

Monastic precincts could be very large, as at Canterbury or Durham, and were sometimes walled, as at St Davids, Lichfield, Salisbury, Lincoln, Wells and Evesham. Many of these monastic houses doubled as cathedrals, and these too were sometimes surrounded by large precincts (figures 10 and 28). During the twelfth century it became increasingly difficult to find space for new precincts in most towns, and thereafter new monasteries had to be content with suburban sites; however, their importance and wealth might attract new growth to the suburbs.

The mendicant friars were the final influx of religious orders into medieval towns, and they became established in most towns in the mid thirteenth century. Their mission was to preach to the people in the market place and, as mendicants, they did not require nor could they afford large churches or precincts. Instead they usually operated from houses in the centre of the town. Later, many friaries were granted money to build their own churches, and small precincts were sometimes created within the town or on new sites further out. It is unfortunate that the sites and extent of many religious houses are unknown; indeed some are known only from documents, while others have been destroyed and built over.

Just as with churches, the monasteries, hospitals and friaries depended directly on the surplus wealth of the town; and if the foundation, number, size and growth of these institutions can be ascertained, they can provide a further indication of a town's prosperity at different periods.

9
Suburbs

Suburban growth began surprisingly early, especially outside defended towns; Winchester already had suburbs in the tenth century, and such areas became an increasingly common feature during the eleventh and twelfth centuries (figure 31). It is not always easy to be precise about what constituted a suburb, especially in towns without a ditch or wall. Their growth was usually piecemeal, though occasionally they were planned; such suburbs were often called 'Newlands', and there are examples at Lincoln (figure 28), Gloucester, Pershore and Banbury. Where the building of a town wall cut through existing tenements, as it did at Hull and Ludlow, some unlucky burgesses suddenly found themselves suburban dwellers, which was not always a good thing in those days (figure 22).

Most suburbs grew either because there was no room for further development inside the town, because a new development needed a large area of land, or because certain activities were not welcomed within the town. Specialised markets such as those for cattle or noxious trades such as tanners and blacksmiths were sometimes located in the suburbs, as well as any activity needing a large space, such as archery butts or fullers' premises. Most later monastic precincts had to be suburban because they required a large area of land which was no longer available in the town itself. As we have already seen, the date of foundation of an extramural monastery or leper hospital will show how far the suburb extended at that date.

Suburbs typically grew up along the major approach roads to the town, clustering around the gates or the entrance to the town; they may or may not have come under the jurisdiction of the town. Often they had their own chapel, and a few larger suburbs had their own parish churches. Occasionally some towns had a complete commercial reorientation in which a former suburb became the town's new centre; this seems to have happened in Hereford, Leicester, Lincoln and Northampton. Keene (see 'Further reading') gives ten detailed examples of substantial suburbs, though he restricts his study to those which developed outside town walls. He notes that some towns enlarged their circuit of walls to enclose suburbs, whilst others were protected by lesser defences such as a ditch. Further, he notes how large

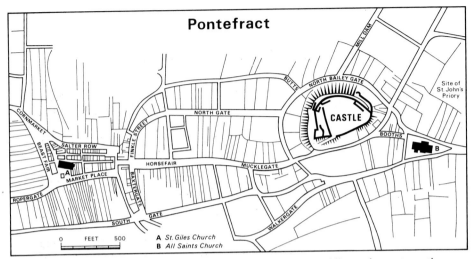

31. Pontefract: All Saints church marks the original village, whilst to the west are the Norman castle and borough, and then the extramural market of Westcheap, established in 1255, virtually a borough in its own right. (After M. Aston and J. Bond, *The Landscape of Towns*, Dent, 1976.)

some of these suburbs became; about 40 per cent of Winchester properties lay outside the walls in 1148. In general, though, the inhabitants of most suburbs were among the poorer people of the town, including many of the town's labourers; such people seldom feature in the town's records, and we cannot hope ever to know much about them.

10
Property boundaries

Fundamental to the rights and freedoms of the medieval burgess was the right to hold property in the town, and this usually meant an area of land known as a burgage plot. However, there was great pressure on space within the town because most people wanted a frontage on one of the main streets so that they could attract customers for their goods, produce or services. In fifteenth-century Gloucester virtually all the tradesmen, dealers and shopkeepers lived and worked on the two main streets, and competition for space was so fierce that many tenements were subdivided.

Thus in order to try to give everyone at least a short frontage on a main street, the house plots were narrow in width but of much greater depth from the road (figures 12 and 32). Each plot would usually have had a house on the street frontage, and the rest of the plot would have been taken up with outhouses, workshops, livestock enclosures or gardens. There was normally some sort of access to the rear of the property, perhaps by a back lane or alleyway.

Few medieval houses survive; most were built in wood (timber-framed, filled with wattle and daub) and were prone to fires or simply succumbed to the ravages of time. Fires were frequent in medieval towns; Pershore Abbey and a large part of the town were destroyed in 1233, and a further forty houses were burnt down in 1288. Thus for various reasons houses were frequently rebuilt, in whole or in part. Archaeological investigation has revealed further detail of town houses; some were constructed parallel to the street, but where plots were narrow or had been subdivided houses might have their gable ends facing the street.

A few houses were built in stone, usually in later medieval times; but only the richest members of the community could afford such buildings. Examples can be seen in Bury St Edmunds, Norwich and Lincoln; only three such houses survive from before 1200 in Lincoln, and all have been linked (either in medieval times, or since) with Jews. Another type of construction was a timber structure with stone cladding; this was a compromise, making the building more fireproof than using wood alone, but less expensive than building in stone. Some medieval buildings have survived inside later accretions; the outside of a building

52

32. Warwick: such typical narrow burgage frontages are usually well preserved, unless there has been large-scale modern redevelopment.

may hide a great deal, and roof timbers can be the oldest part of a house. More detail on town houses can be found in Colin Platt's *The English Medieval Town*.

The 'Great Rebuilding' of the years around 1600 replaced many medieval buildings, but as each house was rebuilt individually, the property boundaries tended to survive, and thus the plot layout usually survived remarkably intact from medieval times until at least the nineteenth century, if not until today. This has been well illustrated by the study of a single block of properties in Alms Lane, Norwich, by Atkin and Margerson (1985) (figure 33). Since the late nineteenth century, the redevelopment of more than one plot at a time has become increasingly common, destroying the physical record of the boundaries. Fortunately we have many detailed town plans, and in particular the large-scale Ordnance Survey plans which usually predate these changes (figures 3, 16 and 20). It is better to use these plans to make any measurements of the plots; they show the burgages before the last century of changes, they are certainly accurate enough to yield good measurements, and the whole of every plot can be seen and measured, something which is extremely difficult and time-consuming to achieve on the ground. Measuring just the plot frontages with a tape is a rather pointless exercise.

Most plots seem to have been laid out in standard widths, using the perch as a unit. Much confusion has arisen over the different units; rods and poles are also often mentioned. Strictly, the standard pole is a unit of length of 16½ feet, or about 5 metres; a perch or rod is a unit of area, being a square pole. The first complication is that the word 'perch' is commonly used instead of 'pole' as the unit of length; that tradition will be continued here. The second problem is that customary measurements seem to have been in use in certain areas, and locally the perch (pole) can vary between 10 and 24 feet (3 to 7.3 metres).

One can easily imagine newly planned parts of a town being laid out using measuring ropes, with stakes marking the plot boundaries. The rectangular shape almost always adopted would make the job easier, not requiring any surveying to be done. Some new town charters specified standard plot sizes; in Salisbury they were to be 3 by 7 perches, and in Stratford-upon-Avon the larger size of 3½ by 12 perches (about ¼ acre or 0.1 ha). In both cases the smaller length was the street frontage.

At Stratford, Terry Slater has shown how the layout of the town and the plots was affected by pre-existing tenements, roads and fields; many plots followed the slight aratral (reversed S-shape) curves of the former ridge and furrow patterns of the

33. Norwich: plot reconstruction. The Alms Lane site, showing the continuity of plot boundaries. Left: the site *c*.1400, consisting of three main tenements. The rented houses on each are single-storey clay and timber structures with thatched rooves and simple chimney arrangements. Right: the site *c*.1720, now very crowded, with all the street frontages built upon and small warehouses and workshops in the yards. The house at the bottom right was a textile merchant's; the others were rented to weavers. (Drawings by Martin Creasey from Atkin and Margerson, 1985; by courtesy of the Centre of East Anglian Studies, University of East Anglia.)

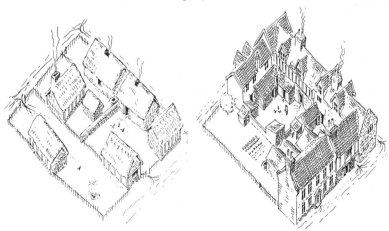

open fields, and the planners thus avoided having to level the
site. The plots were deliberately orientated so that as many as
possible faced on to the main streets rather than the less
important ones. Once the pattern was established, Slater notes
how the original plots were subdivided by the first burgage
holders. One corner plot at the junction of High Street and
Bridge Street, facing on to the market, had an original frontage
(on two sides) of about 13 perches; it was soon divided into seven
smaller plots (figure 34). Here the standard burgage rent was 12d;
any smaller amounts will usually represent subdivisions and can
be spotted in surviving rentals.

Subdivision or amalgamation of plots was common, and the
eight hundred years or so which have passed since the original
plots were laid out have left us with a variety of plot shapes and
widths. Indeed, few plots of the sizes mentioned in documentary

34. Stratford-upon-Avon: burgage plot subdivisions at the junction of Bridge Street and
High Street. The large plots were subdivided by their early tenants (Slater, 1987), and
the Ordnance Survey 25-inch (1914; reprinted by A. Godfrey) shows further alterations.
Fractions indicate proportions of original burgages. (After Terry Slater of Birmingham
University and Alan Godfrey Maps of Gateshead.)

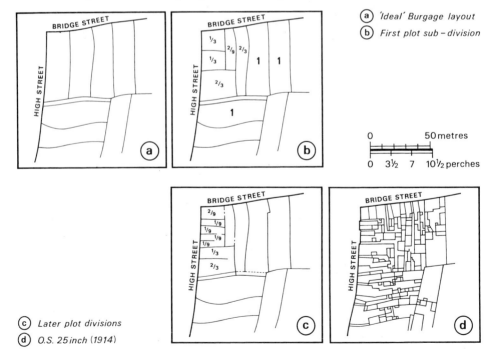

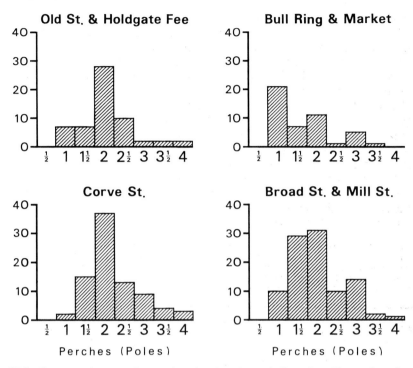

35. Ludlow: most burgage plots are in units of perches or half perches. The smallest plots are in the town centre, and the largest are along the main north-south road.

sources have survived intact. We are now left with a pattern somewhat removed from the original, yet by study and measurement of all the plots it is usually possible to attempt a reconstruction of the medieval layout. Moreover, certain areas of a town may have particular patterns of plot layout and width, representing areas laid out at a particular date. In Ludlow, a study of the plot widths in four areas of the town revealed that two areas have similar distributions (Old Street & Holdgate Fee and Corve Street). These streets are the original north-south road through the town, and the plots may all have been laid out at a similar date (figure 35). The graphs for the other areas of the town are quite different.

The layout of a town's burgage plots is fundamental to the study of the town plan, but it also needs to be combined with details of changes in ownership, occupations and buildings as revealed in the written and archaeological records.

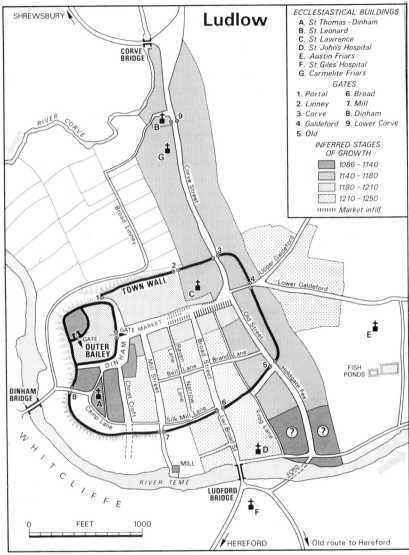

36 Ludlow: medieval growth. By combining the historical evidence with that in the town's layout, this alternative sequence of urban growth can be proposed.

11
Ludlow: a case study

Ludlow is one of the more famous of English medieval towns and has been studied in some detail, notably by M. R. G. Conzen and D. Lloyd (see 'Further reading'). This brief case study will outline the history of the town's growth and then look at the features of the town plan in the order in which they have been described in this book.

In the Domesday Survey the only local reference is to the manor of Ludford, and the origins of Ludlow town lie in the building of the castle in the years around 1090. Some early references have already been noted in chapter 2; it is clear that the town came into being during the twelfth century.

The principal surviving medieval structures are the castle and town walls (including Broad Gate), the chapel of St Thomas in Dinham and the parish church of St Lawrence. There has been very little archaeological work in the town, although the Carmelite friary has been excavated and the site left open to public view. The town has a poor cartographic record, though the Ordnance Survey 1:500 plans of 1885 are invaluable; several extracts have already been seen (figures 17, 20 and 26).

Site

The castle was built on the western end of a prominent ridge overlooking the river Teme (figure 36). It was one of a series of castles along the Welsh border road, strategically placed at this important river crossing halfway between Hereford and Shrewsbury. A town grew outside the castle gates, and it was effectively a planted town, although there is no direct evidence of any deliberate plantation. The town parish was carved out of the parish of Stanton Lacy, though the parish of Ludford has an odd detached area north of the river (figure 37). As the strategic and defensive functions of Ludlow declined, it found itself well placed both for north-south traffic along the Welsh border and for trade (notably of cattle) between Wales and the towns of the English Midlands.

Plan layout

Ludlow's plan, so often described as a grid, is clearly nothing of the sort. The area south of the market simply has three wide parallel main streets (Mill Street, Broad Street and Old Street) which are connected by a cross-lane and separated by back lanes, one of which was called Le Narrow Lane in medieval times (figure 15). Old Street was the original Marches road and pre-dates the others by many years. Another back lane may have existed between Broad Street and Old Street, and in Dinham the plot boundaries of Christ Croft suggest another lost street (figure 17). The town has at least four quite distinct plan units, and the town's layout evolved over many years; there was never any master plan for its design, but it grew by means of planned and unplanned additions.

Streets

The original main road through the town (Corve Street/Old Street) must have existed before the town; it probably crossed the river downstream of the present bridge, leading directly to the old road to Hereford. The building of the new bridge in the early thirteenth century brought the traffic up Broad Street, which was no doubt laid out at the same time. The street is cigar-shaped, reaching a maximum width of 23 metres (75 feet) (figure 14). Mill Street is equally spacious, and Corve Street also widens just north of the town wall; all were probably used as market areas.

Defences

The castle (what is now the inner bailey) was built in the years around 1090, and a settlement called Dinham probably came into being on the slope to the south of the keep (figure 5). The castle was small and could have provided very little defence for the town until the outer bailey was built about a hundred years later. Part of Dinham must have been obliterated to make way for this development. The new castle gates faced eastwards and a new market area was established along the crest of the ridge.

The town walls were not begun until 1233, some two hundred years after the town's plantation; murage grants continued until 1304. The walls are joined to the castle outer bailey; they take advantage of breaks of slope, particularly on the northern side of the ridge, and were surrounded by a ditch elsewhere. They almost certainly bisected the then existing town in three places, cutting across Corve, Old and Broad Streets (figure 20). On the other hand, Mill Street, which led nowhere in particular, probably developed after the wall was built and effectively stops at the wall. The wall can be traced on the ground or on maps for most of its length; the only section where it is totally missing (even in the property boundaries) is just north of Old Gate. At Galdeford Gate two roads converge on the missing gate, and at Corve Gate the road narrows dramatically as it enters the town. Of the gates, only the massive Broad Gate survives (figure 22). There was probably another gate or bar further north in Corve Street to control entry to the market there.

Markets

The main market area was clearly along the ridge stretching from the castle as far as the main north-south road; the junction here was called the Bull Ring. The market was infilled, beginning probably at quite an early date; the rows were in existence by 1439 when their names included Alutarri (leather), Pannares (bread) and Carnificum (execution, no doubt the butchers' row) (figure 26). The market may well originally have continued at its full width all the way to the Bull Ring, but the area south of the parish church has since been much encroached upon, making the present King Street very narrow. To the south, Pepper Street probably marks the original market frontage. All the other wide main streets were probably used as markets too.

Churches

The chapel of St Leonard in Corve Street is known to have been in existence before 1186, that of St Thomas in Dinham in 1190, and in 1199 the parish church of St Lawrence was rebuilt and enlarged; their dates of foundation are not known. The further enlargement of the parish church in the early fourteenth century shows that the town's growth was continuing. The later religious foundations were St John's Hospital (*c*.1220), the Austin Friars (1254), St Giles' Hospital (1267) and the Carmelite Friars (1349); all were in peripheral locations.

Suburbs

If suburbs are defined as urban areas outside the town wall, then Ludlow had four, one even stretching across Ludford Bridge. But as three of these areas probably existed before the wall was built, it is rather dubious to regard them as true suburbs. Nevertheless, the later religious houses are all located outside the walls, and Corve Street may have had a market.

Property boundaries

Ludlow has well developed burgage plots which can be divided into at least three distinct series (figure 35). Those around the

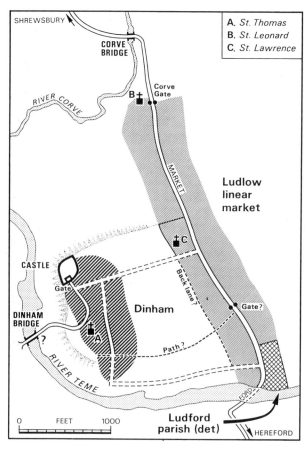

SHREWSBURY

CORVE
BRIDGE

RIVER CORVE

B + Corve Gate

MARKET

Ludlow
linear
market

CASTLE

Gate

Back lane?

Dinham

Gate?

DINHAM
BRIDGE

?

+ C

A

Path ?

RIVER TEME

0   FEET   1000

Ludford
parish (det)

FORD

HEREFORD

A. *St. Thomas*
B. *St. Leonard*
C. *St. Lawrence*

37. Ludlow: the town may well have looked like this *c.*1180. It is certain that almost a century after the building of the castle there is little or nothing in the way of defence for the burgesses.

market and the Bull Ring are narrow, the most common width being 1 perch, reflecting the pressure on space in the town centre. In Broad and Mill Streets the plots are typically either 1½ or 2 perches wide (figure 20), whilst those in Old and Corve Streets are most commonly 2 perches wide, perhaps suggesting that these two streets were laid out at the same time. There is a curious reference to burgages existing near the chapel of St Leonard before 1186; it is very surprising to find urban settlement at the northern end of Corve Street at such an early date.

Town growth
     The obvious and traditional view is that the Dinham area was settled first, then the formal market area was laid out, followed

by growth south from the Bull Ring along Old Street; the Broad/ Mill Street unit came fourth and most of the rest is of later date. There are a number of problems with this outline. The first is the unusual site of the parish church; it is not in the usual prominent position. Second is the existence of a detached portion of Lud-ford parish north of the river, near the old ford; there must have been some sort of settlement here, as the castle and its early town were half a mile (0.8 km) away, unable to provide any protection or services. Third, there is the early existence of burgages and a gate at the northern end of Corve Street.

Thus an alternative view of Ludlow's growth is equally ten-able. In this scenario, the early castle was established, and Dinham grew up outside its gates; soon after, a straggling trading settlement grew up along the main north-south road, from the ford right up to St Leonard's. The parish church in such a settle-ment would have been in a very prominent position, on the crest of the ridge, visible from everywhere in the town. The town at this stage (c.1180) might have looked as depicted in figure 37, with two distinct settlements. There was no point in the towns-people hoping to hide inside the castle if there was a Welsh attack; there was not enough room. However, the castle was later enlarged, and outside its new gate a large market area was laid out. Finally, the Broad/Mill Street plan unit was added to accommodate the growing trade and traders, diverting the main route up Broad Street, and leaving Old Street to decline. The town walls were added after most of the town had been built, cut-ting through the town in several places. Proof of this view of the town's growth might be obtained only by archaeological excava-tion of the castle's outer bailey, to see whether Dinham did once exist there, and at various sites along Corve and Old Streets, to date more precisely the growth of the town along this road.

Conclusion

Perhaps the message of this chapter, and indeed of this book, is that we should try to take a new and detached view of all the available evidence and not to be bound by commonly accepted or obvious solutions. Throughout, this text is peppered with words such as 'usually', 'most' and 'often', but we must always be pre-pared for the exceptions to the rule. A final thought on the study of medieval town plans paraphrases a maxim from geomorpho-logy: 'complexity of urban evolution is more common than sim-plicity.'

12
Further reading

Aston, M., and Bond, J. *The Landscape of Towns.* Dent, 1976.
Atkin, M., and Margerson, S. *Life on a Medieval Street.* Norwich Survey, 1985.
Barley, M. W. (editor). *The Plans and Topography of Medieval Towns in England and Wales.* CBA Research Report 14 (1976).
Barley, M. W. 'Town Defences in England and Wales after 1066' in M. W. Barley *op. cit.*
Beresford, M. W. *New Towns of the Middle Ages.* Lutterworth Press, 1967.
Biddle, M. *Winchester in the Early Middle Ages.* Clarendon Press, Oxford, 1976.
Butler, R. M. *Medieval York.* Yorkshire Architectural and York Archaeological Society, York, 1982.
Carver, M. *Underneath English Towns.* Batsford, 1987.
Conzen, M. R. G. 'The Use of Town Plans in the Study of Urban History' in H. J. Dyos (editor), *The Study of Urban History,* 1968.
Griffiths, R. A. (editor). *Boroughs of Mediaeval Wales.* University of Wales Press, Cardiff, 1978.
Hindle, B. P. *Maps for Local History.* Batsford, 1988.
Historic Towns in Essex. Essex County Council, 1983.
James, T. *Carmarthen — An Archaeological and Topographical Study.* Dyfed Archaeological Trust, 1980.
Keene, D. J. 'Suburban Growth' in M. W. Barley *op. cit.*
Kelly, S. 'The Economic Topography and Structure of Norwich c.1300' in *Men of Property.* Centre of East Anglian Studies, Norwich, 1983.
Lobel, M. D. *Historic Towns.* Volume 1, Lovell Johns, Oxford, 1969. Volume 2, Scoler Press, 1975. Volume 3, Oxford University Press, 1989.
Lloyd, D. *Broad Street* (Ludlow). Studio Press, 1979.
Morris, M. *Medieval Manchester.* Greater Manchester Archaeology Unit, 1983.
Ordnance Survey. *Viking and Medieval York.* 1988.
Palliser, D. M. 'Sources for Urban Topography: Documents, Buildings and Archaeology' in M. W. Barley *op. cit.*

Platt, C. *The English Medieval Town.* Martin, Secker and Warburg, 1976.

Slater, T. R. 'Ideal and Reality in English Episcopal Medieval Town Planning'. *Transactions of the Institute of British Geographers,* NS 12 (1987), 191-203.

Steane, J. M. *The Archaeology of Medieval England and Wales.* Croom Helm, 1984.

Winchester, A. *Discovering Parish Boundaries.* Shire, 1990.

Index

Page numbers in italic refer to illustrations.